WHAT A REAL WOMAN WANTS, WHAT A REAL WOMAN NEEDS

A Gentleman's Guide to Understanding Women

Madena Williams

authorHOUSE®

AuthorHouse™
1663 Liberty Drive
Bloomington, IN 47403
www.authorhouse.com
Phone: 1 (800) 839-8640

Published by AuthorHouse   07/27/2016

ISBN: 978-1-5246-1975-6 (sc)
ISBN: 978-1-5246-1974-9 (e)

Print information available on the last page.

This book is printed on acid-free paper.

Introduction

In many cases, a person has to stop in life and take a good look at himself or herself. On many occasions this practice isn't done. Whether you are a man or woman, you may feel as if it's better to look at someone else's faults than your own, and that really isn't true.

This book was written for men only to help them learn what real women's needs are, how to understand real women better, and most of all, how to understand themselves. It also provides information about to how to properly attract the right woman. It is my goal to inform and explain how some females act the way they do. Everything you read is not inconclusive. Many situations in this book have been researched, and some are from personal experiences. Being well informed about how to proceed with the next phase of your life is always a good start.

In order to fix what is stopping you from choosing the right woman, you have to look at everything about yourself. You must lay it all on the table; write it down with pen and paper. Once you have done this, you may be surprised at what you find out about yourself. If you just got out of a bad relationship, then you need to do one of the following: Either take a break from relationships, or start out a new relationship as just friends. Starting out as friends is the best way to start a relationship. After you have accomplished this goal, then proceed slowly. Time is not of the essence when choosing the right friend.

Chapter 1

Fix the Relationship You Have—Or End It (Be Honest, Not Foolish)

When in a relationship, many times both of you will have some sort of disagreement that may result in a strong negative environment. The situation may result in either a light or a strong disagreement. Beware when tempers flare; that is when the demon comes out—in one of you or both of you—and the result is often violence. When this happens, one of you has to have the good sense to leave. At the very least, you should drop the subject until you can discuss the matter calmly. In some cases, you may have to have a mediator to help you discuss the problem more calmly. If it ever gets to that point, then that will be the time to go over the roles both of you played in the crisis. This process will help you find the basis of the problem. You can then work together to find a solution and stick to that solution so that the situation does not repeat itself.

It is important that you know how to keep a *disagreement* from becoming a *fight*. A disagreement happens when there is a difference of opinion, and that is all there is to it. Now, if one of you wants to take it further, there could be something that needs your attention. You may ask yourself, *Why is she so defensive?* or *Why is she getting upset over something so trivial?* Open your eyes and ears! Maybe there is a reason she is feeling guilty. Maybe you just struck a nerve. Don't forget to check yourself; you may be at fault also. When in doubt, think about the old saying that "two wrongs don't make a right." So whatever you're checking her for, make sure you're checking yourself too—and don't blame her for what you're hiding. Remember, for every action, there's a reaction. If you are arguing and the tables turn on both of you, that's because *both of you are wrong*. Why? When tempers are flaring, anger will take the situation to the next level. This is why you have to be cautious in your battles of words. You just may say something you don't mean, but those words *will* escalate the disagreement into something neither of you is ready for. This is why you need to learn to cool your temper. When you can do that, the results will be much better, and the make-up part won't be so bad.

Now, when you are making up with your mate, keep sex out of it. Sex is a tool that is used for the wrong reasons. It's not supposed to be used as a make-up tool because the situation that you and your mate are experiencing is not supposed to be heavy duty. When you anger your mate, you need to solve the problem. You also need to allow time to heal—a moment, a day, or even a week, depending on the argument you just had.

Now, some females can be downright stupid and take the situation much further than it should have been taken in the first place. (I will talk about that later in the chapters.) Men always want to make up with their mate using sex, and that is the wrong move. You need to consider how she's feeling, not how you are feeling. You need to help each other recover from the bad feelings that were created when you were in battle. Yes, I agree that is easier said than done, but you have to find a way to overcome the situation. Please be creative. A good woman loves to know that her man really is sorry; that makes her love him even more. You are the man, so take charge and bring the relationship back to a positive normal.

Now, let's talk about how to stop pointing fingers at one another. This happens a lot of times in relationships, and it also causes relationships to stay in a catastrophic situations. In order to avoid pointing fingers, you both have to be adult enough to admit to your own faults and then devise a plan that will eliminate the negative attitudes you are each causing the other to have. Once you put this plan in motion, you should have fewer outbreaks of negative emotions. In some cases, you both could be at fault in the squabble. This happens when both people are disrespectful, inconsiderate, thoughtless, untruthful, or controlling. With these issues that I have mentioned, your relationship becomes dysfunctional, and that can lead to domestic violence.

You have the ability to repair your relationship. The question is, do you really *want* to repair the relationship? A relationship is never easy. Going through the good times is easy; it's the hard times that make it challenging. Before you decide to throw in the towel, take a look at the whole situation. Review everything the relationship has gone through, and then look to see who the biggest troublemaker is. With this method, you have to be honest with yourself; there will be no room for denial. If you are causing this friction to go on, then stop it. If she is causing the friction in the relationship, then you must have a talk with her. Offer to come to an agreement of peace. Remember, when working out this agreement, you both have to agree to do the same things. If both of you are at fault, it will take both of you to make this work!

She has to be as willing a participant as you are. She has to be part of the healing process. It took both of you to create this problem in the first place. You caused each other to defend yourselves, and before you knew it, the battle had begun. Now don't get me wrong. You're going to have squabbles, but it is up to both of you to keep it respectful. If by some chance you see that she isn't doing what it takes to repair the relationship (especially if she was the one to mastermind the problem in the first place—be honest), you need to start doing some deeper thinking. You need to prepare to make an exit.

Note: In some cases, this is harder to do because you may have obstacles in your way. These obstacles could be a bank account (in both of your names), children, property, and other circumstances. The list can go on and on. I will speak later on how not to get caught up in these hindrances, and how not to play "husband and wife" when you're not married.

Repairing a relationship takes time and effort by both parties. You have to ask yourself if you are willing to put time into the repair. Is she willing to put time into the repair? Don't use the ridiculous excuses, please: "But we have great sex together" or "Her body is too fine for me to let go." Well, if you're going to use that kind of excuse, know this: those reasons are responsible for the predicament you're in now. Never base your relationship on sex or a woman's anatomy. When you do that, you will have a bad relationship every time. Do yourself a favor and use the *right* head.

Knowing When to Call It Quits

Let's say you did all you could to fix the relationship. I mean, you bent over backwards to change and do everything right by the book. But none of it worked, and things are getting worse between you. Not only that, but your mate is just being a pure devil. She isn't showing signs that she wants to even keep the relationship, and you are seeing a side of yourself even you haven't seen before. Well, when this happens, you know what you should do: call it quits—and mean it. Pack up and get out. If you are living in your house, advise her that she has to leave ASAP! Sever the relationship before something illegal happens—someone goes to jail for domestic violence, or someone goes to prison for murder or attempted murder. She isn't worth your freedom being withheld. If the relationship has become that dysfunctional, or if either of you is guilty of domestic violence, you must accept the fact that you no longer have a relationship. Do what must be done and leave! Don't be stupid and fall for those innocent, emotional behaviors that she will pull on you. Think, man! She hasn't been innocent all this time (and neither have you), so what makes you think she has changed? Not only that, what makes you think she is willing to change her attitude toward you when she hasn't done so all this time? It is a trick; don't fall for it. Some women see that some men are easy and stupid. So what these women do is play these men, and by the time these men realize the picture wasn't what they thought, it's too late. The female is on her way, smiling like the cat that caught the canary. Don't be one of those men. Keep on walking—and don't turn back.

Financial Options

One thing to remember when splitting up with your mate is that there will be a financial cost for the event. No matter if you're married or single, have children or not, or if you have a bank account together or not, there will be a cost. This is what we call a "relocation fee." Let's talk about being married. If you don't have any children, then the fee is much lower. Without children you can see to maybe spending $100 to $200 per week, maybe more. If you don't have a place to go to, then you may have to live in a motel until you can find an apartment. Then you have to buy food for the duration until your next check. I know you're not going to pay the bills at your previous home, but keep in mind that, if she wasn't working, you may have to pay. Even though you've left, you're still married, and you should still carry out your duties. I'm just stating what you should do unless there is another man in the picture; that draws a different conclusion.

If children are involved and they are yours, then send your soon-to-be-ex money for the children. When you send the money, send it by mail and make sure it is a money order. In the memo area, write "For the children." This proves that you are taking care of the children. You are creating a paper trail, and if she takes you to court, you can prove to the judge that you have been taking care of your children since you left.

Now, if the children aren't yours, then it is what it is. Do what you know you should do in that situation. If the children aren't yours but you have been taking care of them all this time, then you need to continue to take care of them. Just because you and your woman, whether married or not, have broken up, that doesn't mean you should make the children suffer as well. They had no part in the circumstances of your relationship. Some men want to get back at their wives or mates by treating the children

5

badly. The only thing you are doing at this point is making things worse for yourself. Just think—if those children really loved you, and they treated you as if you were their biological father, and then you start pushing them away with your antics to get back at the mother, those children will begin to hate you, and they could take that hatred into adulthood. Ask yourself, do you really want that to happen? It's something to think about.

Now, let's talk about relationships in which there is no legal attachment whatsoever. If you are not married, there are no children, and there is no jointly owned property (this includes boats, cars, houses, land, or even a business), then the separation will be less expensive. You will still have expenses, but they won't be so extravagant.

Remember when I mentioned a relocation fee in the section about marriages that are breaking up? Well, the same goes for the breakups of unmarried couples. No matter what condition you're in, you are going to have to spend money—period. There is no way out of it when you're breaking up with your mate. Whether she is a wife or girlfriend, money is going to be spent. Let's look at the darker picture of this information that you need to remember. Let's say you are moving out of your home, leaving behind your wife or girlfriend. You've packed your bags and taken everything you own with you, and left nothing behind but the dust on the floors. Okay, at this point you've decided that it is truly over. Now, did you prepare for what she is going to do next? Did you think that it was going to be a quiet breakup? Did you think that she wouldn't make a fool out of herself over the fact that you've left her? Think again, my friend. Some women will do just that and more. You see, it doesn't matter who is at fault; it's just that it's actually happening, and she can't deal with it. This is where it can get more difficult. You have to get use to the idea that she is thinking like this: *I am losing my mate to another woman (if this is the situation). I'm losing extra income for paying the bills. I'm going to be lonely. There'll be no one to talk to.* She may try to see where you are living at so she can cause trouble. She may go to your place of work and start some trouble. She may find your vehicle and vandalize it. The costs for dealing with all of this is included in the relocation fee, because if she does damage to your personal property, then you will have to spend money to replace it. You may work for a company that doesn't keep employees when trouble comes to the establishment concerning their personal lives. Do you get what I'm saying now? It may be true that you don't have a relationship with this type of woman, but it won't hurt to keep this information in your archives—the back of your mind. If another woman is involved, then you really need to get ready to go through hell.

If you are going through a breakup, then I wish you luck. No matter who is at fault, it affects your emotions, the way you think, your daily living, your health, and your finances. We never think about these things because we all think for the moment. In a relationship, you want to trust the one you gave your heart to, and sometimes we overdo the trusting. In your next relationship, make sure you have chosen, to the best of your ability, the one you really want. It is going to take time to make sure that you made the right decision, but you have to spend the time, and you have to be alert to all areas of your feelings. Play it smart, and next time, think with the head between your shoulders.

Chapter 2

Once You're Out, Don't Go Back

Sometimes we come to a point in our lives when we find ourselves lonely, and we make poor decisions about the people we let into our lives—or back into our lives. This chapter is for those gentleman who are confused about whether or not you're making the right move when you decide to let someone into your life, or back into your life.

When a woman wants you back in her life, she will use techniques that will make you almost say, "Okay. Maybe we can get back together and give it another try." Bad move! There are a lot of reasons for not rekindling the relationship.

Let me start with this: You see, if you can recall the reason that you broke up with your wife or girlfriend in the first place, you should be able to realize that your relationship was *not* repairable. You may have tried hard, and she may have tried hard to keep the relationship together, but it just wasn't working. So, because of that, together, you didn't repair anything; both of you left the situation unhealed. Whatever the problem was, it tore the relationship apart, and you are about to re-expose old feelings because you're just remembering the good times you had together. You're not remembering the bad times. The bad times are the reason you're not with her now. Look at all the money that you've spent because of the separation. I have just mentioned some of the things you may have gone through, but of course you know only too well the extent of the devastating hit it caused both of you. The question you need to ask yourself is, *Do I want to go through all that agony again?* If you go back to the relationship you had then remember this, whatever broke up the relationship before will happen again. If you had sex with each other, that is no reason to go back. If you have been civil to each other for a long time, that is no reason to go back either. Both of you may have been dating since the breakup, and things have been wonderful. Okay, so what does that mean? I will tell you: it just means that both of you have been having a good time, and that is all there is to it. You need to understand what I'm saying, and not be hard headed. Don't get me wrong; you do what you want to do. You are a grown man, and you choose your own battle, but if you want to understand what the hell is going on with some of these females, then you need to listen and learn.

If you decide to risk going back to the old relationship, then you need to address together what happened in the first place. Then you both have to calmly resolve the problem, and make sure it is truly resolved. Don't just say you're sorry (and I mean both of you); rather, understand why the problem existed. When you do analyze the problem together, make sure you solve it so it never happens again. If by some chance you get into an argument, don't bring back up what broke you up in the first place unless one of you fell into that old behavior again. If this happens, then that means one thing: the one who is bringing that problem up again lied when he or she said, "I forgive you." Yes, you know that lies will break up a relationship and, yes, you are back to square one with the situation that broke you up in the first place. This is why it is best not to go back to a previous relationship. Save the extra heartache and start out fresh.

Chapter 3

Figure out What Went Wrong (Mapping Out)

Now that the relationship is completely over, you must take the time to analyze the situation and determine the actual cause of the breakup in the first place. In your analyzing, don't just blame her; you had a lot to do with the situation as well. In any relationship, both partners are responsible for the success or the failure that takes place. Pointing fingers at one another doesn't help in the recovery. In order to have a successful understanding of what happened with your wife or girlfriend, you have to look at her side as well as your side. Then come to a conclusion about how you are going to make it better next time with a different mate.

In your analyzation, you need to go all the way back to the beginning of the relationship and start there. Always go to the beginning and follow the trail from there. Go through each and every moment of the relationship, including the good times and the bad times. Pay attention to the good times that turned into bad times, and the bad times that turned into good times. This has to be done because you are trying to protect your beliefs, and decide whether or not you have to change.

This action will help you in your relationship with the next mate you pick. (Don't go off on that adventure too soon!) In your analyzing, determine whether the change started with you or your mate. I caution you not to do your analyzing in your head because you won't get all the answers you're looking for. You need to take paper and pencil and start writing down all the episodes that happened, good or bad. Write down what caused each one, who started it, and how it ended. Make sure you have two columns on that paper. Label them "What Happened?" and "How Did It

End?" Under "What Happened?" include what happened, when it happened, and who started it all. Under "How Did It End?" include how it ended, when it ended, and who ended it. With this method, you can pinpoint when the problem started, and you can sometimes actually see for the first time who may have started the downfall of the relationship. And you may be surprised at what you find! When you're doing this method of analyzing—or a similar method of your own invention—it is important to be truthful to yourself and put the blame on the right person. Also, make sure you're in a calm and serene mood. Yes, you're going to feel angry at what happened, but you need to stay focused and remind yourself that it's over. Remember, you are just trying to figure out what actually happened, how it happened, and how not to let it happen again. Keep in mind that for every action, there's a reaction.

For your convenience, I'll supply you with questions to help you start your analyzation. Use these questions and their answers to pinpoint only the problems that actually occurred. You must be honest and truthful with your answers. Lying to yourself will result only in failure to improve yourself and your future relationships. If you were wrong, man up to it!

Here are the questions you need to answer about yourself and your behavior:

- Were you always inconsiderate of her feelings?
- Did you always take advantage of her?
- Did you give respect to everyone else except her? Did you play around on her?
- Did you give her affection and spend much-needed time with her?
- Were you both dysfunctional?
- Did domestic violence play a role in your lives?

Now answer the same questions about her and her behavior.

With this method, you are trying to pinpoint the actual problems that created the turmoil in the relationship. This is an important step because you have to make sure these issues don't come into your future relationship. You will be able to identify destructive mindsets and behaviors and stop negative actions before they happen again.

The answers to these questions should give you a good start in your process. The one thing you need to do is to be honest with the answers. You see, sometimes we get caught up in our own agendas, so we forget to show that extra caring emotion that men and women need to feel. Sometimes men and women need to hear "I love you." Do things that show your partner you love her—make positive comments about his or her appearance, show compassion and understanding. You will learn in the chapters to come how important it is to feel love—to feel that your mate loves you, understands you, and most of all, trusts you. Good luck in your analyzing!

Chapter 4

Cheating on Your Woman Isn't a Mistake

"I made a mistake." It's a tired cliché that both men and women use when they cheat on their mates. They say it in order to make amends. Sometimes it works, and sometimes it doesn't; it all depends on how bad the cheating was, and the length of time it was happening. This chapter will relate to the previous chapter in that cheating is one of the major reasons that couples break up. Now, with that being said, let's continue with the phrase "I made a mistake." The dictionary states that a *mistake* is an incorrect statement or action that is the result of not paying attention, having poor judgment, or not having enough information.

Now on with the lesson. When you're cheating on your woman, it's never a mistake. You meant to cheat—you thought about it, and you planned it. You went through the process of getting the other woman's number. You planned the actual rendezvous. And there you have it. That, my friend, isn't a mistake. Just because you are a man, that doesn't mean you have to— or you have the right to—cheat on your mate. (That's another cliché.) If you are going to do something as foolish as that, then you have no business making a commitment to any woman, good or bad.

Here are some of the lame excuses men make to convince themselves to cheat on their wives or girlfriends: She's on her period. She's sick or had surgery. She cheated. She won't play along with my fantasies. She doesn't like oral sex. She doesn't please me anymore. Yes, men base their stupidity on these reasons. There is no real excuse that a man can use to cheat on his mate. If you feel you need to give excuses to cheat, then you need to end that relationship. Sex is not supposed to be the main reason for you to be together. Sex (with proper protection) should be a bonus to the arrangement, not the main attraction. Sex doesn't provide powerful stability for the relationship. It only serves as pleasure enhancer, and that is the only quality it possesses. It has nothing to do with what the relationship really needs in order to be successful.

Being intoxicated is another weapon a man uses as an excuse for his cheating. Don't you know a woman can see that coming before it comes out of your mouth? Yes, let's talk about the drinking that caused you to cheat. You see, this is what is wrong with your flawed logic: You make many decisions while you're sober. You made the decision to drink, and you picked the people you wanted to drink with. You know how you are when you drink, and you were aware of what you were doing when you made the decision to cheat. As I said before, there is no real excuse for cheating. And there are pitfalls: Did the female have protection? Does she have a disease? Will she make trouble for you such as getting pregnant?

So it is safe to say that nothing "just happens" because, when a man decides to cheat, it's not a mistake. A word of advice: Cheating is cheating, and if you can't maintain a monogamous relationship with your partner, then be man enough to sever the relationship you're in, and save yourself a lot of heartache.

Chapter 5

Stop Listening to Your Buddies

Some men—not all—have buddies who will give them the wrong advice when it comes down to using common sense. Many times your buddies can't support their own relationships let alone advise you about yours. To listen to their advice is a major mistake, and following their advice will guarantee the failure for your relationship. You need to think about the type of friends you keep.

The reason I make this statement is that I believe you may choose your friends for good company to hang out with. Well, in some cases, hanging out and having a serious conversation are two different things, and you may not get the true answers you are seeking to the questions you ask. Another side of sharing information with your buddies is that you could be feeding them valuable information that could help them get with your woman. If you start telling all the details of your relationship, your so-called buddy could take notes and use the information to get to know her in a sneaky way. Think before you speak.

Now, with that being said, let me take this train of thought deeper. Say, somehow or other, that you and your woman are having big trouble keeping your relationship in a positive manner. You are desperate to get some sort of relief for the misery you're having. So you decide to talk to one or two of your buddies about the situation, and you actually give details about what started the dysfunctional environment. Here are two scenarios that could develop when you start talking:

Scenario one: You tell your buddy about your problems, and he informs you that he doesn't know what to tell you, or he wishes he could help you. So you spilled your guts for nothing. You trusted that your friend would ask what went wrong so that your answer could help you pinpoint what the problem is. But you are unaware that you just gave your friend information he could use in two possible ways.

The first possibility is that your friend shows he's concerned about your problem, so he actually pays attention to your venting. You think that he's got your back with regard to what's going on, when in actuality he's collecting information for himself so he can approach your partner from a different angle—sneak in from the backside and make a move on her without you knowing. That action could very well break up the entire relationship altogether.

The second possibility is that your friend doesn't care about the problems you're having, and because he doesn't treat his own woman right, he gives you some solutions that will, without a doubt, tear your relationship apart if you do what he suggests. Always remember that your drinking buddies are not the best people to ask when you need advice. You may want to hang out with them, but hanging out with your drinking buddies may give the wrong impression to other people. Not only that, but did you ever think that your drinking buddies might be partly the cause of your relationship going south?

Scenario Two: Now, let's hope that you have some good male friends with whom you have good ties, and they can offer you some good suggestions about how to fix your relationship. After you have tried all you could to salvage the relationship—you both admitted your faults and tried to make amends—and things are just not working, and the attraction isn't there, then it is definitely time to sever the relationship and move on.

Before you go looking for another relationship to get into, you need to just have time to yourself to get over the ordeal from which you have just been freed. Always use common sense about having time to yourself. It isn't necessary for you to get into another relationship right away. It is important for you to have quality time for yourself. Don't be in a rush to be involved again. By all means, take this time that you have to look at what went wrong in your previous relationship, and make sure that it doesn't happen again. Be fair in your analyzation, for it will help you the next time around. When you do start looking for a possible mate, remember that some decent women are in bad relationships, which they are trying to get out of themselves, and it's not easy to get out of those relationships at all. These women can go through the same experiences you've just gone through to get out of a dysfunctional relationship. Just a reminder—don't try to get involved in someone else's bad relationship, for you will be asking for something you can't handle. In just about every relationship there are lies and deceit, and the trick will be to determine who is telling the truth—maybe one of them is lying and cheating, and maybe both are. So don't be stupid; stay out of it completely.

Chapter 6

The Lord Is Speaking to You Even When You're Not Listening

Looking for answers elsewhere when you have had the information within you all the time can make you look foolish. This happens when you don't explore your own avenues for the answers to the questions you having been holding since your misery started. You see, many times we go through times in our lives when we don't like the answers that come to us for that special problem we have been experiencing. No matter what the answer is, how hurtful it may be, it is possibly the answer to your situation. You have to own it and then change it by settling the situation. Then turn it to a positive outcome to make it better.

When trying to solve your problem isn't working, then maybe you need to take it to a higher power. You see, there are men who actually pray to God about their situations and then let Him handle it while they continue to work on the problem. Sometimes you just have to admit that you need help from Him in order to stop your misery. Is that happening to you?

When analyzing your situation, be fair and honest to yourself about whether or not you were the main cause. If you were the cause of your problem, then find every way you can to fix it. After that, make sure it doesn't happen again. This is your big chance to learn from your mistakes and prevent them from happening again. When you learn from your mistakes and make sure they don't happen again, you are growing up and becoming more mature.

When you let love rule you, you become your mate's puppet. You become her fool when you let love blind you from truths that will destroy your will, your manhood (no, I don't mean

18

your penis), and the common sense that you are supposed to use to defend yourself against those who try to destroy you. Love is an emotion that has to be controlled on all levels so you can safeguard your heart, your feelings, and most importantly, your common sense. God did not put you on earth for you to let people (especially females) walk all over you; you are not meant to become someone's henpecked footstool. Learn to become a real man by standing up for what is right. Be aware of your surroundings, and take care of yourself in a positive way. Also, don't follow other men who want to show brute strength all the time. These men don't have the common sense of a jackass. Learn how to use your mind, and concentrate on the correct way to solve problems in a positive way. You must learn to rule love, not let love rule you. If a female is taking advantage of you, I wonder why.

Tunnel vision is the perfect enemy for everyone! It is one of the main causes for breakups in relationships. I am talking about love relationships, business relationships, friendships, and family relationships. It can even affect how you make important decisions in life. Let me explain what tunnel vision is. If you have tunnel vision, you see only certain aspects of a certain situation. You see things that are the most obvious to you and your situation, and that is all. When you are supposed to see the whole picture, you don't, so you make a decision based on half-truths instead of the whole truth. When you are looking at any situation in order to make the correct decision, you have to look at the whole situation and not just parts of it. You have to analyze the good parts as well as the bad parts in order to get the full picture of any situation. Then, and only then, can you attempt to make the correct decision.

Use this method for choosing the next female you invite into your life: Stop listening to negative advice from people you know or don't know. You have to understand all aspects of your situation. Take responsibility for what you have done or caused, learn from your mistakes, and then move on. Remember, a mistake is something you don't know you're doing. The final outcome was something you wouldn't have expected. Or you have found out that what you truly believed in was not the right situation for you. If you had to think about an action and you knew that it was going to cause a problem, then that could not be called a mistake. If you played around on your wife or girlfriend, that was not a mistake. So in this lesson, don't use the word *mistake* to describe what you did when you purposely took action.

Regardless of what your spiritual beliefs are, you need to get all the negative thought patterns out of your mind and stop listening to all the negative advice you may be getting from your friends and family members. Start listening to the Lord. If you have some positive thoughts in your memory, capitalize on them and start praying to the Lord about your situation. The only thing you should remember is that the Lord will not steer you wrong. He will give you the answers and show you the right way to go. Perhaps some of your friends and family members want to see you fail, but He doesn't want to see you fail. The Lord wants you to succeed, and He wants you to stop causing yourself so much unnecessary misery. Think about it.

Chapter 7

Having a Relationship Is Never Easy

Everything in this chapter will let you know what probably went wrong in your previous relationship, and what should have happened in order to have made it a successful arrangement. So, let's explore these ideas with more than an open mind. Remember to be honest with yourself and to stop pointing fingers. Bury the "She did this and she did that." You let it happen because you accepted what she was doing for quite a while. You are now trying to rebuild your life, your feelings, and your confidence by trying to figure out how to find the right woman. It's not easy at all, but I will tell you what to look for, and how to recondition yourself so that, when you come across her path, you will be ready to either defend your heart or start your new friendship. Either way, you should be smarter after you have read this chapter than you were before.

Learning to forgive the previous relationship will bring positive possibilities into your life. In your previous relationship, you and your mate weren't right for each other; it is clear that you got together for the wrong reason. Neither of you could possibly have been mature enough to handle the relationship, and your ideas were at opposite ends. This is what caused the breakup in the first place. Of course this is just one explanation for things going wrong. Holding on to grudges will just attract negative females to you, and this will put you into negative situations. My advice is to get over it and move on.

When you have decided to finally forgive and forget, make sure you really do mean it. Don't play a game by saying that you forgive her, and then later on decide to bring the issue back up again. That means you lied and you really didn't mean what you said. You are causing your own pain at that point, and you are going to bring those same feelings into a new relationship. That will cause your relationship to fail before it gets started. And by all means, don't talk about the old relationship to your new female friend; doing that could give your new friend false signals.

Look, everyone wants a relationship that runs like a well-oiled machine, but that isn't going to happen until you find the right mate and you go through the ups and downs a normal relationship goes through—together. Stop with the games (I mean both of you) and start with understanding, respect, communication, compromising, and investing time in the relationship. These elements are the perfect ingredients to put into a strong base for the beginning of a lasting relationship. Going through the years in a relationship, you have to make sure that neither of you is taking advantage of the other. You are not lying to each other. You are keeping other people out of your relationship. And you are not telling your private business to your friends and family. Your relationship is personal, so keep it personal.

Avoiding domestic violence will give your relationship an A+ grade, and I'm talking about physical, mental, and sexual abuse. Remember, when you start your next relationship, whether it's just a friendship or a more serious commitment, you don't own her and she doesn't own you. Once you have understanding, respect, communication, compromising, and investing time, then you can begin to develop a well-oiled machine of a relationship. Don't be fooled; it is going to take years for the relationship to be set and running by itself. Remember, a relationship takes work, and love isn't going to be enough (not by a long shot).

Once you are together, you both have to remember that you are a team, and as a team you must work together toward positive goals for each other. This action is for serious relationships only. If you aren't working together toward positive goals for each other, then the question would be, why are you together in the first place? My point in saying this is to make you think. You enter into a relationship with a person to share your life. If you don't care enough about that person to help her work toward her goals, she may not care enough about you either. If this is the case, it is possible that neither of you is ready for a serious relationship. I'm just giving you something to think about, and that's all. Always remember that, if you are a team, you can work together to achieve positive goals.

Once you are together, keep others out of your relationship. Having others in your relationship will damage it, and it will end. When I say others I mean family members, friends, and strangers. If you have a spat (which is normal), then keep it between you and your mate. Make sure, if you can, that she does the same thing. Your relationship is personal; remind her of that.

You must understand that it won't be smooth all the time. Both of you have to work to keep the waters smooth and calm. You will disagree on some things, and that's okay. Both of you need to learn how to compromise and come to a positive agreement. It can happen if you have the right woman (make sure you get the right one).

Teach Her Your Needs and Wants

While you are anticipating how your new relationship is going to begin, you need to concentrate on letting her know what your needs and wants are. When getting to know her, pay attention to what she is saying—and what she is not saying. In some cases, you can show her what your needs are. Here are some examples: Be on time for dates (leaving on time to get where you are going on time). Always show respect for yourself and others. Be considerate of others, and her especially. Use caution before you speak. These are just some of the actions you need to follow within yourself in order to train her to understand your needs and wants.

It's mandatory for you to be mindful of her needs and wants as well. As long as her needs and wants are respectful to others as well as herself, then respecting them should be doable.

Always remember, your needs and wants are just as important as hers are. Always discuss what you want—don't assume she knows—and review with her what you feel your needs are. Keep games out of the mix when discussing mutual needs. All of this should take place at the beginning of the relationship—within the first month as you get to know each other. This is when you need to make sure she knows some of your desires. You can reveal the rest of them during the second and third months, as by then both of you should know if you want to proceed with the relationship.

Some women can be quite strange. Not all women are alike; each one is different. Even women who share the same characteristics are still different. You need to seriously understand that you know only the women you have been with. You can't say all women are the same, because that would be a lie. You can't say you know how all women are. Remember, you know only the women you have been with.

Some women are mysterious, and some are like an open book. Some women are weak, and some are strong. Some are leaders, and some are followers. I am saying this so you will see what type of female you might accept in your life. It is vital that you know what type of female you're keeping company with. Once you have learned what type of woman you have, it should be easier to have good communications with her, and your intuition should be good with regard to approaching your newfound friend.

Leaders and Followers

Here's something to think about. In the previous paragraph, I mentioned that some females are leaders and some females are followers. We must look at the differences between these types, and how these types of females can impact your life.

Let's talk about women being leaders. Now, I'm not talking about a leader on a job, for example; I'm talking about a leader in personal values. A leader is a person who takes charge of himself or herself and life's situation. This person can even take a relationship and steer it in the right direction, and above all, take on responsibility in a positive way in order to receive a positive outcome.

Now, women who are followers tend to be a lot needier. These women need someone to lead them in almost everything they do in life. They often have low self-esteem and depend on others for strong support. Pursuing this type of female could be bad news for you. Here is another thought I want you to think about: A woman who follows others can follow the wrong crowd of people and insert herself into certain cliques in which other females are always in someone else's business. This type of female feels secure in these cliques because she wants to always be led, and usually it is in the wrong direction. This type of female tells all of her business to her friends, and yes, she will tell the business between you and her if you decide to bring her in your life. This female doesn't use common sense because common sense isn't common with her at all. This type of female also portrays a busybody attitude. She is always in everybody else's business, and always gossips about others. (No, not all females share this type of character.) Also, she never takes care of her own business, and she will bring trouble to herself as well as anyone who is with her. This type of female is bad news my friend, so beware and play it smart.

Providing Support for Each Other's Beliefs

Backing each other up on certain issues is the beginning of building trust and confidence between each other. Certain undesirable issues that may arise in life sometimes are more tolerable if you know you have your mate's support. A real woman wants to be supported by her mate. She also wants to come home and be able to have good conversation with her mate. It is important for her to know that she actually has a real friend she can begin to trust, someone who can later become her confidant. Now, you should receive the same courtesy from her. You should realize by now that I am saying this so you can build a solid base for a good relationship. Remember, every good relationship has to start with a good solid base.

Domestic Violence—Stop it before it Begins!

I want to start with you. I want you to be man enough to look at your own character and see what type of domestic violence gene you have within you. Domestic violence can consist of mental, physical, and sexual abuse, all of which lead to dysfunctional relationships. Here are some signs that may indicate a person is dysfunctional:

- The person is always untruthful and deceitful.
- The person is quick and always ready to start an argument.
- The person finds fault with everything others do.
- The person throws objects, sometimes with the intent to damage others.
- The person always cusses and is defiant.
- The person has no respect for himself or herself or even others.

These are just some examples that you can look for in a person to see if he or she is dysfunctional. Remember, dysfunctional behavior leads to domestic violence.

Protecting Your Relationship

Once you have made the decision to be a couple, it is going to take both of you to protect the relationship. Now, you may already know that, but there are a lot of men who don't understand that it takes both of you to actually protect the relationship. It is not just up to you; she has to protect it as well. Keep an eye on her and yourself. Yes, I said you too. The reason is that you can easily slip back into your old ways, and those ways may have been the reason your previous relationship didn't make it. Remember, don't give your full trust in any new relationship. Never!

Now, in protecting your relationship, you need to watch everyone, from friends and family members to old girlfriends. Don't be stupid. Don't hand out a résumé of your newfound relationship. Do you know what I mean when I say *résumé?* Let me explain. You see, a résumé is a document that lists past and present work experience. Potential future employers use a résumé to understand the background of a person applying for a job. Well, telling your friends and family members details about your new friend that shouldn't be told is like giving them a résumé about her to them. You know how some men are—they tell their buddies if they've gone to bed with a woman, and then they tell what they did in the bedroom in order to show off. Don't get mouthy like the female follower. Remember, whatever a mouthy female does, the mouthy male does the same. Bottom line, keep other people out of your relationship.

Compromising Is a Must

When you are in a relationship, you must learn how to compromise with your mate. It isn't going to be smooth sailing all the time. Disagreements are going to happen sooner or later. So you both must come to a compromising agreement occasionally so that things can run smoothly. This is actually another form of respect and a show of concern for the other person's beliefs. It may be an adjustment, but compromise is a necessary ingredient for a good relationship.

Understanding Your Mate

When you find a good mate, you have to take good care of her as well as yourself. Yes, she has to understand you and your beliefs, and you have to understand hers as well. It is a two-way street. When you find a good woman do well by her. If you have won her heart, she will take good care of you, so don't do anything stupid. Make sure you understand what she wants from a man, and always give her your attention. Notice her when she comes into your sight. Always be glad to see her. Don't be afraid of her if she brings out the best in you. You might be surprised how some men actually want good women, and when they get a good woman, they don't know how to treat her. My advice to you: If you want a good woman, make sure you deserve one. Just because you think you deserve a good woman doesn't mean you actually do. So, fix up your character before a really good woman comes along, and do right by her in your future relationship. After all, no one wants to be alone in life.

Love Is Automatic When Everything Is in Place

This is my favorite part. You see, you hear so many people saying "We fell in love at first sight." or "I just met him (or her), and I'm in love." These sentiments do not even come close to the truth. When you hear someone making statements like these, they're not in love with the person; they have fallen for the things the person does or how the person looks. There is no way you can fall in love with someone you don't fully know. In these next few paragraphs you will begin to understand what I am talking about, and then you will have a better understanding of what really happens when you meet a person. You will understand what you are truly falling for and why you are attracted to that special person. You will also learn why you should have your guard up at all times. Let's begin the journey, shall we?

There are many reasons that a person begins to have feelings for another person. When you've found that another person has shown a friendly attitude toward you, you respond the way you normally do—hopefully, with respect—and she responds in a positive way. You immediately probe her personal life by asking if she has a boyfriend or husband. Now, if the answer is no, then you proceed to ask her out on a date. When you are on the date, you really need to pay attention to what she says, and most importantly, how she acts. You will also determine whether or not you want to proceed in the relationship and see her again. Now, being a man, the first thing you probably pay attention to is her anatomy. If you like what you see, then you get to know her. This is normal for a man when approaching a female. Caution: Remember what I said about tunnel vision in Chapter 6? Just because a female has the right body, that doesn't mean she has the character you want and need. *Think with the right head!*

Once you start the dating process (if you make it pass the first date) you will see if her beliefs are compatible with yours. If you are compatible, your feelings toward her will become strengthened. If everything goes well, with every meeting and every conversation, you will be strengthening your emotions for each other. Now, please remember that you are going to have some disagreements. Each of you may experience some anger. Remember to maintain respect for her and remind her to do the same. Calmly and respectfully discuss what made you angry, and guide her to do the same. If she truly wants to be with you, then she will comply. (Kind reminder: Keep your personal life off Facebook. You relationship is your business and no one else's. Also, make sure Facebook isn't her top priority, because it can ruin a relationship.) Remember, as you grow together, respect each other and keep communication open at all times. Love will fall into place automatically. There is no reason to rush, so take your time and create the right relationship.

Chapter 8

Love is Never First

Many times people say they love someone, and they don't even know that person. Let's explore the constantly misused definition of this emotion. One thing you must realize—when you start saying you love her because of her body, or the way she talks to you, even the way she acts toward you, you need to ask yourself, *How can I love a person when I barely know her?* The truth is that you lust after her. You admire the way she walks, the way she wears her hair, the way she wears her clothes, and so on. These are just the beginning attractions that inspire the process of the two of you being together.

This is where you get jammed up, and yes, I am talking about tunnel vision. Tunnel vision is one of the main reasons a man gets himself jammed up in a dead-end relationship. Tunnel vision allows you to see only part truths. It appears that most men have tunnel vision. When choosing the right woman, you have to be alert at all times. Never let your guard down. Sorry to say, while you're looking for a good woman, female predators are looking for a good victim. You could be the next victim! So never let your guard down. A predator will do what she can to get what you have. She'll even pretend to be the best woman she can just to use you, and you won't know what hit you. Remember, you may think you know a person, but reality says you don't.

I also want to remind you not to dismiss red flags that start going off in your head. There is a strong reason they're going off, and you need to pay attention to them. When you see a red flag about any situation, there is a good reason to put up your guard and keep it up until the situation has been resolved. As always, don't let tunnel vision give you partial truths. Bust through tunnel vision, and you will see your true answers. Then use that answer to handle the situation in a respectful, positive manner, and keep violence out of it.

It is important to see a woman for who she really is, especially in the beginning of a relationship. Knowing what you're getting yourself into is the basis for a good relationship. Just as you do, a woman will hide what she doesn't want you to know. There are some things you don't need to know about her past or present. Yes, I agree that her past or present condition could be a problem, but you need to wait at least until the second or third month before you start inquiring. When you do inquire, begin with a calm, casual conversation about her past. You can say something like this: "You know, we've been seeing each other for a while now, and I really enjoy being with you. If you are ready, I want to take our relationship to the next level. I must ask, do you have anything in your past or present life that I need to know about? Anything that will affect this relationship of ours?" I strongly advise that you pay special attention to the way she reacts to your question. Also, if she chooses to remain involved with you, keep your guard up, and be alert at all times. Remember, it's still early in the relationship, and you need to watch how much trust you give her.

Are you infatuated with her body or the way she treats you? Caution: You can't answer yes to both because you haven't been with her long enough. Now, if you say her body, then you have a big problem. You're setting yourself up for failure. Just because the female has a great body doesn't mean she will treat you right. That great body will not give your relationship the stability it needs in order to survive. You need to pay strong attention to her character: Is she a fake? How does she treat other people? Please understand that the way she treats other people will give a strong indication of the way she will treat you. Now, I'm not saying you should find a female who isn't attractive to you; I'm just stating you should consider picking a female for her ethics. Also, watch out if she drinks. She may be a different person when she drinks, and she may turn out to be the kind you don't want to be around. I'm giving you this advice so you can think with the right head. Don't let stupidity and tunnel vision ruin your life.

If you're mature enough to understand this paragraph, then you won't have a problem with what I'm about to say. When I say think with the right head, I strongly believe you know what I'm talking about. For those of you who don't, then let me explain so you will know the difference. On many occasions, a man might see a woman with a nicely curved body and start thinking sexual thoughts. This thought pattern intensifies when liquor or drugs are in a man's system. This scenario often leads to unwanted babies. Yes, sexual diseases are a certainty, and both you and the female have opened up a new series of problems (as if you don't have enough). This is what I call *thinking with the wrong head* (meaning your penis). Some men who see a female with a nicely curved body actually stop and think before they get themselves into trouble. These men are thinking with the right head (the head between their shoulders). Thinking with the right head gives men the advantage over females who may be trying to deceive them. No, not every female is out to deceive a man, but men need to use common sense where common sense isn't so common. The first step in using common sense is to use the head between your shoulders: Think before you act! The second step is to assess her and analyze her motives. Be smart and stay alert. The third step is to not let tunnel vision turn you into her victim. Right or wrong, don't let the wrong head rule; the results could be disastrous.

Making unnecessary babies is not a mistake. Stupidity and recklessness result in out-of-control actions that can have stiff penalties. Yes, there are men who actually protect themselves from an event that will forever change their lives. And there are those who will be reckless till the day they die. Many females don't have the self-respect to safeguard themselves from pregnancy. So you, being the male, need to seriously take responsibility and safeguard yourself against any female. Females lie, so even though your sex partner says she is using protection, make sure you do the same. Using a condom will not only protect yourself from pregnancy, but will also protect you against sexually transmitted diseases. Just because your sex partner looks disease-free doesn't mean she really is.

You may ask, "What if she never said anything?" Well, stop trying to get out of the situation. If you didn't have protected sex, it is possible you made her pregnant. Yes, she may be sleeping with other partners, but that is beside the point. I'm talking about you and only you. I just gave you one strong, real-life scenario. Some pregnant females actually do not tell the guy that she is pregnant. So be smart and protect yourself. Stop making up excuses for why you can't wear protection. Remember all the reasons you should protect yourself when having sex. Also, you need to think about oral sex. If you can get sexual disease when having intercourse, you can also get the same infections and diseases with oral sex. Getting high, buzzed, or drunk is no excuse, because you made the decision before the act.

Another thing that causes infections is an inadequately cleaned penis. Clean your penis, scrotum and buttocks correctly. This particular message is for those men who are not circumcised, or men who have too much skin around the head of the penis. Pull the additional skin toward yourself and clean the entire area thoroughly. Too many men clean only the top of the skin that covers the head of the penis. Because the penis is not clean, it can smell and it can become infected. The infection can be passed along to a female sex partner, who might wonder where the infection came from. Keep in mind, this is just one of many ways to get infections and diseases. This is why cleaning your penis correctly is important. Cleanliness shows a man's respect for himself and his sexual partner.

Chapter 9

Identify Your Shortcomings, and Then Fix Them!

Look at your character. Are you a kind person? Are you difficult to be with? Are you always looking down on yourself or others? These are just some of the characteristics you need to pay attention to. If you are a gentleman, then don't change. This is a quality you need to embrace because it is one characteristic a good woman looks for in a man. Next, look at your bad habits to see what needs to change. Don't become lazy in changing your character for the better. The bad habits that you had in your past relationships may not be tolerated in your new relationship. Whether or not it's a relationship you want to take from the friendship stage into the personal stage, it's always wise to get rid of bad habits that could destroy what you're trying to build. Also don't settle for less. You deserve to have a good, quality relationship. Sometimes we can't see anything wrong with ourselves, but that isn't entirely true. There is always room for improvement and for making corrections that will change our character for the better. Once you have made up your mind to change, take it day by day, minute by minute and hour by hour. Practice your change in character every day of your life, and don't let friends or family put you down for your efforts. Consider your self-improvement project to be personal, and keep your mouth shut. Do not look for other people's approval to do positive things in your life. Have confidence in yourself, and if you have positive religious beliefs, always use prayer to help the process of change along.

To make the best of your quest, you must identify the positive and negative things you do. As always, this is private, so keep your process to yourself. It is important to use paper and pencil to start your procedure. Never analyze your character in your head because you will miss a great deal in your analyzation. On your paper, in one column, list the positive things about your character; in the other column, list the negative things. When you are finished, look at the two lists to see which one is longer. Take note of what you see, and then start working on the negative side. This is what you want to fix first. Even if you think it's not that bad, nine time out of ten times it *is* that bad. Here is a small project for you: Look at the negative side more closely. For each characteristic, pay attention to how much you are bothered if you experience the same characteristic in others. Once you see how you feel when you observe the attitude or characteristic in others, you will prepared to make plans to fix it in yourself.

Now for the positive side. Look at it more closely and figure out what actions can be improved upon. Once you have made your decision, start the process immediately. Please don't undertake positive actions just to impress someone else. That would mean that you're a fake and cannot be trusted. Be yourself, and don't add actions to your character you can't keep up. (Don't become an actor when you're not getting paid for it.)

Remember how your actions affected your previous relationship. Keep in mind that I'm not talking about your previous mate; I'm talking about you only. Take a look at the list below and see if any of the points fit you. Be honest and don't lie, because if you do, then you're lying to yourself only.

- Were you selfish?
- Were you too demanding?
- Were you uncompromising?
- Were you untidy around the house, including your car?
- Did you spoil your mate by being too giving?
- Were you henpecked by always doing what she wanted and never having a say in decisions?
- Did you spend enough time with your mate?

- Were you a perfectionist, domineering, my-way-or-the-highway sort of person?
- Did you show affection outside of sexual encounters?

Note: These questions should help you analyze your behavior. Only by being honest with yourself will your self-analyzing be valuable. If you answer honestly, you will probably not make the same mistakes in your new relationship. Just remember how you were in your previous relationships and figure out how your actions contributed to the failure of the relationship. Remember, it takes two for a relationship to fail. Figure out what happened, and then don't let it happen again.

Chapter 10

Understanding Yourself
Makes the Search Easier

You must become aware of who you have become since your last relationship. Your previous relationship may have left a bad taste in your mouth, and you probably blame most women for your ex's attitude. News flash: All women are not the cause of your mistake in picking the wrong woman. There are other women in society who have attitudes similar to your ex's, but still, keep your blaming in the right perspective. Now is the time for you to heal from your misery. Don't point fingers; stop blaming your ex. You must move on because you can't change the past. If your past relationship has caused you to have ill feelings toward women in general, then you must lose those feelings. The right woman could be watching you acting your worst, and if that happens you will lose your chance to meet a decent woman. Remember, whether you want a relationship or not, you need to work on fixing your attitude for the better. I tell females to stop bashing men, and I'm telling you to stop bashing females. If you do what I suggest, you will have a better chance in picking the right woman. Please know there are no guarantees, but at least you now know how to look for the right woman.

It's important for you to adjust your beliefs if they are wrong. If your beliefs are wrong, your assumptions are probably wrong. When you are carrying negative thoughts all the time about any situation, those thoughts invite tunnel vision into your life. Do you remember what I said about tunnel vision? It allows you to see only part of the truth instead of all of the truth. My friendly advice to you is to stop carrying strong negativity about things you can't change. Start concentrating on how you're going to make your life better, and yes, you do have control over that.

Don't be so trusting. Don't open your arms to greet the female predator. Remember when I said never let your guard down? Well, when you actually keep your guard up, you can stop the female predator in her tracks. If a female predator infiltrates your life, she will take you for everything you have. Now, you may be hard headed and say that you don't have anything that she can take. That isn't so, for you have no idea what she is coming after. All I'm suggesting is that you think smart and guard yourself. These types of females are good at what they do, and you can be caught off guard. Don't be so sure of yourself, because you could be the perfect victim for what she is after. Don't get caught with your guard down.

Protect your faith, and don't lower your expectations. You have the right to be happy, but you are going to have to work at it. Please open your mind and pay attention to what I am about to say. It is important that you understand my message. Now, it must be understood that, in order for you to start on your road to happiness, you are going to have to come out of your comfort zone. Your comfort zone is a place where you feel comfortable at all times. It's a place where you can make decisions that will enhance your personal space. If and when you decide to share your space and your life with another, you are going to have to make sacrifices in order to accommodate your decision. You will most likely have to leave your comfort zone in order to get things you don't have. Your comfort zone is your home. You have to leave your home to go shopping for food, to go to work, to go on trips to other cities, and to meet people. The reason you have to go to these places is that these places will not come to you. So you have to go out and get food so you don't go hungry. You can have the comforts of cooking or eating inside of your comfort zone. Well, you have to do the same thing with trying to seek a good woman. You can start your search as you carry out your regular activities. The best way to meet someone is to keep your eyes open while running errands. Use the same method when you're out having fun, or just out engaging in your hobbies. My point is, meeting a person could happen at any time, so just watch out for it.

Let me remind you that you are being watched when you are out in society. Because of this, you need to remember to be on your best behavior. When you're out in public minding your own business and acting your best, females will notice you. As I have said before, if you're a gentleman, you need to embrace that character. It actually makes you better than other men who are not. A real woman loves it when a gentleman holds the door open for her. A real woman loves it when a gentleman gives her a respectful compliment. You see, it is regrettable that some females don't know how to take a compliment from a gentleman, and yes, that is sad but true. Please keep in mind that these women sometimes aren't expecting the politeness you're providing, and that makes it even more noticeable. By all means, don't read into it more than what it is, for it's just what it looks like, and that is two respectful people being respectful to each other—that's all.

Chapter 11

Keeping Your Character in Check

As I mentioned in the last chapter, if you're a gentleman, make sure that you embrace gentlemanly behavior always. As far as self-improvement is concerned, being a gentleman gives you a head start on your way to establishing good character. Being a gentleman doesn't just extend to females; it also extends to other men, and to society in general. Being a gentleman is another form of being courteous and considerate. That's all it is, don't read more in to it. Please remember, just because you dress like a gentleman, that doesn't mean you are one. I say the same about the females—just because a female dresses like a lady, that doesn't mean she is one. She must embrace the character of a lady, and you must embrace the character of a gentleman as well. Be aware that there are a lot of imitators out there, so you are going to have to pay special attention to both dressing and actual character. Just to let you know, true ladies will have the same character all the time. It is true that they have bad days too, but the good thing is that true ladies always get back into character, and that's what makes them so special.

Decent women are always watching. They are dressed in pants, dresses, jeans, or respectable shorts with shirts or blouses, or in suits, dresses, and other respectable clothing. These women are not dressed in dresses and skirts with a nice blouse all the time. Do you remember what I said about having the character of a respectable lady? You may not find a respectable woman dressed in shorts so short that you can see her butt cheeks sticking out below the pocket. A true lady doesn't wear anything that revealing. She lets a man use his imagination, and that is something most females don't do these days; some do, but there are many who don't. Remember, a decent woman has the character of a lady. I'm just reminding you—a lady is a respectable female who has respect for herself and for others. She treats others the way she wants to be treated, and she expects the same courtesy from those around her. She is polite, and she can get her point across without acting like a full-hearted bitch. (The dictionary definition of *bitch* is a disgruntled female.) When you make a female angry, she can show her thorns, and they can be sharp. A decent woman has thorns as well, and she can expose them when necessary. A decent woman is not weak at all, so don't ever think that she is. She can be a strong-willed person, and she is a respectable female.

If you are into religion, then you need to make sure you stay in religion. When I say "into religion," I'm talking about following God's rules and regulations. You don't have to be super religious to serve God. You don't have to change your legal name to one of the names in the Bible. I'm so tired of men changing their names to biblical names and then behaving just as hellishly as they did before they changed their names. These men change their names to strong religious name like Solomon, Nicodemus, and other biblical names. These men are extremely hard headed, and they need to understand that it isn't the name that makes the man. What makes the man are the actions that you do in life, and one of the most important actions that these men don't do, is to let God guide them toward a positive outcome in life. Now, with that said, you have to understand that, if you're going through troubles in life, you are supposed to be experiencing them. One of the easiest things in life is to get into trouble, and once you get into trouble—depending on how bad and how deep it is—it could be hell to get out. You are supposed to learn from your mistakes, and each learning experience is supposed to make you stronger for the next event you will face. There will be no rest. Every day you live and breathe, there will be a learning experience. Whether you encounter something you have never seen before, you never heard before, or you never felt before, it is a chance to learn something that you didn't know the day before. You may be the type of person who's an atheist, and that's on you. Religion is free will. I am not here to try to convert you. I'm just explaining how to get through life and how to pick the right friend (or mate).

I want to give you another thought that you may not have considered. When looking for a real woman, don't think of it as looking for a mate. You need to think of it as looking for a friend. You may grow closer than you think by just being friends at first. Men and women need to be friends before they become more involved. Go on dates as just normal friends with no strings attached. This will lead to spending more time together. While you are getting to know your new friend, don't give any type of signals that might indicate that you want to be more than friends. In some cases, you may need to slow her down in case you are being too good to her, and that could become a problem. I understand if you don't want to have a mate at the moment, but all the information I'm giving you is helpful whether you're looking for a mate or not. You just might want to be friends so she can go to her home and you can go to your home with no strings attached. That is a fine thought and is doable. But please remember that the information I'm giving you is for understanding a real woman only.

If you decide to go to an online dating site, you really have to watch what you do. Your guard must be up at all times, and you can't trust anyone. I picked this chapter to tell you about dating sites because those sites are loaded with female predators. You will not know who they are, and it will be hard to sniff them out. Some of those female predators are stupid, and if you're up on your game, then you will be able to catch them in the act. If you are a respectable man with a gullible character, then you are the perfect victim. Just because a person looks innocent, that doesn't mean he or she is. Just watch yourself. What seems to be too good to be true usually is. So don't believe everything you see and hear. If she is rushing you on anything, especially a bank account, then something is wrong with that female.

Chapter 12

How to Spot a Decent Woman

Okay, you have been looking for this information, and now I'm giving it to you. Please understand that I had to get you prepared for this section, because you always have to recondition yourself before you get into a new relationship. Even if you don't want another relationship, it is always good to keep a good perspective on your character. Now, in the previous chapters you have learned how to fix the relationship that you're already in. You have also learned that, if you can't fix the relationship, then you must sever the bond. You have learned that there will always be a financial burden attached to any separation. I have revealed to you some of the things that can contribute to the breakup of a relationship, and some clichés that don't make sense. From this point forward, I hope you're ready for any decent woman you may get. Make sure you do deserve one. Decent women are hard to come by, and if you are lucky to receive her presents, make sure you treat her right.

You can find decent women in respectable stores—famous brand-name supermarkets, stores at the malls, and even in the dollar stores. Women you meet in sewing stores could be gifted with crafts. When you see these women, notice at how they are dressed. Remember, they could be wearing skirts or pants or respectable-length shorts or capris with nice blouses, or dresses for shopping. Look for overall decent attire. These ladies will have neat hairstyles. They aren't going to look like Stepford wives, dressed up like dolls. These females are going to look like your everyday decent-looking women, and they will have the character to match. They aren't going to be rude, loud mouthed, overly opinionated.

You might meet some of these women at meetings at work. You might meet them in a restaurant while they are gathering with other females during a girls' night out or a luncheon. You might be surprised where you can find decent females. The next lady for whom you hold a door open could be "the one." Please be mindful that these females could be in bad relationships as well, trying to get out because they made a mistake just like you did. Unfortunately, it happens to the best of us, and on many occasions, it's going to take God the Father to rescue them.

There are other decent women in church, and that is where you really have to watch out for yourself. Church isn't what it used to be, and the females have changed considerably. If you are a religious man, then you really need to include the Father in your search for a good mate. It is true that loneliness is a hard emotion to conquer, and it will cause you to do some of the dumbest actions ever. So because of that, you need help in searching for the right friend who will take care of you and become a good companion. We all need companionship in our lives. A companion stops the loneliness from becoming overwhelming. It is nice to have a conversation for a change that doesn't turn out to be a battle. Now, you know the kind of female who goes to church, but when she leaves, she is the one of the biggest hellions that walked the earth. Stay away from that type of female! As I said before, that type of female will cause you nothing but problems.

Now, if you already have some friends, and they fit the description of decent females, and they are not with anyone, then you need to pick one to have special conversations with. Remember, don't cause problems with these females. It is true that decent females get off track, and they need to be reminded about how to act in order to show that they have some sense. I am just giving you some ideas on what is already there. Sometimes we look to the far ends of the earth for what we want, only to find that what we've been looking for was right under our noses all along. This often happen to us in our daily lives, and this is just something to think about. To have a real woman is like no other experience for a man. She should be strong willed, and at the same time she should be respectable, respectful, tender, and motivated to be responsible. Remember that a real woman will have respect for herself and other people.

So far, you and I have explored dealing with females without children. Now I must touch base on dealing with women who have a child or children. The situation is a little different— and more complex—when children are involved. Not only do you have to connect with the mother, you have you have to connect with the children as well. Don't be nice to the kids just to get in good with the mother. Having a relationship with a woman with children is a big responsibility, and you may not be ready for a giant leap like that. The relationship could involve more problems than you want to deal with. If you never had children, then dealing with them is going to be a big adjustment for you. Those adjustments will include the fact that you will not be number one in the relationship—those children will be. The mother may start to depend on you for support of the children, and your financial responsibility will grow. There is so much more that could happen if you have a girlfriend with children. If you're not use to being a parent, then you aren't going to make it. Believe it or not, there are decent women who have children, so please don't get the idea that decent women don't have kids.

If you meet a woman who has kids, and you're in the friendship stage, then notice how she treats them. Pay attention to how the children are clothed. Are they groomed properly? What is their overall appearance? Also, how does she speak to them? Does she speak normally, or does she cuss at them? Next, how does your new friend control the children in public as well as at home? Are the children as respectable as she is? Does your friend apply good parenting skills with the children? Would you say your friend's family is dysfunctional? Does she spoil her children? These are questions you need to be asking yourself if you decide to take your friendship to the next level.

Please understand when choosing any woman with children, or even just one child, that the process can be complicated. Even if you can deal with children, the situation can, in some cases, be a problem between you and the mother.

Even if you can handle children in a positive way, the relationship can go bad quickly, especially if the relationship is new.

Chapter 13

How to Approach the Respectable Woman

If you feel the need to approach a female, introduce yourself in a respectful way. You may say you know how to approach respectfully, but there are a lot of men who do not. These men ruin their chances the minute they open their mouths. These men who don't know how to speak to a woman properly say some of the dumbest things. Here are some good tips to follow:

- Never approach a female with food in your mouth. Have some class, and approach her in a respectful manner.
- Don't approach a female mumbling. If you can't speak up and enunciate your words then stay away.
- Don't approach a female saying something like "You're looking fine, babe" or looking her up and down like you're trying to analyze a slab of meat. There are a lot of decent women who don't like to be approached like that. You will have lost your chances before you started.

A respectable woman may not like those stupid actions, and if you do these things, you're not a good match for a decent woman. A decent woman doesn't deserve such disrespect, and any man who behaves this way is 100 percent inconsiderate and looking for a bootie call only. Yes, there really are some men who approach women disrespectfully, and these are only a few examples. If you know how to approach a woman respectfully, then do so. Don't be fake about your character; just be real about your intensions when speaking to her. Please keep in mind, if you have to keep up appearances that aren't normal for you, don't start in the first place. Be yourself and don't imitate someone you're not.

When you see the need to approach a female, make sure your body language isn't offensive. Have a nice smile on your face rather than a smirk. Don't walk up to her with your hands in your pockets. With all the male predators out in the world, you don't want to give her the impression that you are one of them. Please understand that the things that I'm telling you are just suggestions that you should consider. As I have said before, every woman is different, and there is a special unique way to approach each one. So please remember, however you decide to approach a female, make it respectful.

Another effort you can make when approaching a woman is to compliment her on the way she wears her hair, or on her smile, her outfit, or even the item that she's buying. All this, if done in a respectful way, can defiantly get a conversation going if there is a true opportunity. Also, if she has a sad look on her face, that just might indicate that you can come in and offer some assistance. You may be the only one who can make her feel a little better. Sometimes a woman needs to hear advice from a stranger in order to give her a new perspective on things. And in some cases, it might be nice for her to have a man's point of view. If you have time, just lend her an ear. Sometimes that can be a conversation starter. She may just need a friend, and you can be true to her by being that friend. You know decent women go through crap in life just as you do. Here is something to think about: Some females don't even know they are decent until a true gentleman shows them that they are. The reason is that they actually made a mistake and got with the wrong person. So their hell began, and with all the heavy stress they've been going through, they can't see the good in life.

Now, if you come across a woman who is married, then you need to bypass her immediately! Let me explain something to you. You see, some decent women are committed to another relationship that they can't get out of. In some cases, unfortunately, they want to have their cake and eat it too, as they say. Don't get caught up in that situation. Just because these women are decent, that doesn't mean they don't make stupid and crazy decisions. Keep in mind that a good man makes stupid and crazy decisions as well, so don't point any fingers at her.

You may ask yourself, *Is her life complicated?* Let me help you. Of course it is if she is married and still trying to let you talk to her. Remember, someone who is pretty or dainty could be as lethal as hell, so watch yourself by thinking with the right head! All women, whether they are decent or not, have a side to them that would shock you. How many times have you heard someone say *"It's the quiet ones who are dangerous"* or *"The innocent-looking ones are the ones to watch out for"*? Well, this is how it is with women. Whatever a man does, a woman does the same exact thing. She may not do it the same way a man does it, but in all realty, women are capable of carrying out the same deceitful actions men do. I am reminding you of this possibility because, for some reason, men sometimes lose their common sense when a woman is involved.

If you hold a woman's company long enough to find out that she is married, but she says she's separated or she's getting a divorce, don't believe what you hear. Even if it's true, do you want to put yourself into that type of tangled web? A woman can lie just like man can, and females can come up with some big juicy ones too. These women sometimes try to get involved with other men so they can try to get the man to take care of the problem husband or boyfriend. Not all women practice this type of deceit. I'm just trying to tell you to watch your back, that is all, and pick the right woman.

If by some chance the female really is divorced, and you somehow want to take a chance on her, then proceed with caution. Have your guard up at all times. Now, here are some questions to ask yourself: Is she close to her ex-husband or ex-boyfriend? Is she always holding conversations with her ex? If they have children together, does the father go out with the kids?

These are just some of the things you can watch if and when there is an ex involved.

Here's a cautionary reminder: Just because she is getting a divorce, that doesn't mean that she or her soon-to-be ex knows how to let go. Even after the divorce, there could be some feelings that are still there. Not all the time, but in some cases it could be a problem. This is why it is best to be friends at first. You can have as many friends as you want. Try to keep sex out of it because that does complicate things a great deal.

Chapter 14

The Right Woman Has Flaws Like You Do

When looking for a good woman, you must remember that there are no perfect women. Every woman has flaws, and you can't be so critical about how a good woman really is. A good woman, in your mind, may be the type of woman who will follow your directions. A good woman, in your mind, may be the type of woman who takes care of the house, bears babies, and stays at home all the time. A good woman, in your mind, may be the type who doesn't complain or even approach you about you stay out all night, or when you do wrong. Well, my friend, if you have all this in your mind, then you don't want a good woman, you want a robot that will carry out your every command. Women like this don't exist in reality.

A real woman will often have an opinion that differs from yours. She feels that her ideas must heard, and in many cases those ideas are good. It's a nice thing to have a difference of opinion because exchanging ideas makes for good conversation. This is the type of woman you want for a good companion. Also, make sure you don't pick a woman who is strong willed. Being strong willed is okay, but strong willed could lead to disaster in a relationship. Being too strong willed will lead to a miserable relationship. Confidence is a good thing, and the woman who is confident will be a good asset to the relationship. Over confidence, however, can result in too many mistakes, and this, in turn, can result in failure as well.

A good woman can teach you by showing you the correct way to do certain things, as long as you don't get to the point where you know everything. (Yes, the same goes for her.)

Madena Williams

Absolutely do not get involved with a materialistic woman! She will wipe out your bank account. Materialism is one of the worst traits a person can have. I hope you are not materialistic, because if you are, then you may not be a good match for any woman. Let me explain what a materialistic person is: A materialistic person must always have certain things just because he or she wants them. Items range from jewelry, clothes, and trinkets to cars, houses, decorations, and so on. The price for these items can be damaging to the bank account, and the desire can wreak havoc on a relationship. In some cases, materialism can destroy the relationship.

Don't ever let any woman tell you what you want for yourself. You are an adult, and you should know what you want—and who you want to be with. Now let's explore the need for you to stay single, but have a girlfriend. Several men have told me that their girlfriends keep pushing them to be more than friends. Now these men who have confided in me stated that they weren't ready to be more than friends, but their women kept pushing them. I told these men something they had never considered: "The female may be a decent woman, but she has strong flaws that will override her character. Regardless of your wishes, she is disregarding what you want for yourself, which makes her selfish. This action is bad on her part because she is pushing you against your will." To the gentlemen who are reading this book, please don't let any woman—good or bad—push you to go against your will for her selfish reasons. Stay in control of your life and let only God tell you what your life needs are.

There are some women who are extremely negative. These women are so negative, no one wants to be around them; neither does anyone want to deal with them. They can treat you somewhat nicely, but to others, they are advocates for the devil. Now, if you pick this type of woman, you will be miserable for the rest of your life. This particular kind of woman will want you to be on her side in any given situation. Right or wrong, she will demand you stick by her beliefs. If you don't give her your support, then she will turn on you. Do not pick this type of woman for a friend or partner. This type of woman is 100 percent dysfunctional, and she promotes domestic violence.

Decent women have little flaws that will get on your nerves. (Remember, you're no better!) Let's talk facts about recognizing other people's faults, and about people not recognizing their own. There are a lot of females who gather together in small cliques. Many times these females make a practice of looking for other people's faults and flaws, and they make fun of them. For some women, this may be a moderate occurrence, but for other women who are powerfully active in talking about others, this is a major problem. You really wouldn't be able to handle the outcome. If these women spent more time fixing themselves, they would not have the time to find fault with other people's actions. Decent females have pride about themselves and do not need to rate other people. Now remember, minor gossip is normal for both men and women.

A good and decent woman will take advantage of you. In some cases she may not be aware that she's doing so. She may be occupied in thought, and it happens, or she may be analyzing a thought too deeply, and that is another way she can take advantage of you. Playing games is another way of taking advantage of you. Now I'm just talking about the decent woman. The games she might play are the games that will manipulate you to get her way. Once again, she will have bad habits just like you do, but that doesn't mean she isn't a good and decent woman. Sometimes it takes a good man to help a good, decent woman to be aware that her character needs improving. You say this to her by actions. Your actions can make a difference if she really cares about you. Another thought for you to remember is that she can be a strong and positive influence on you; she can help you, as you can help her. Together you can become the best for each other.

Chapter 15

What Not to Bring to Your New Relationship (Weeks One through Three)

Attitudes from the Past

It's known that your previous relationship is not your favorite subject, and you don't wish to talk about it. I have given you reasons to re-examine what happened in your previous relationship, to give you clarity about what actually transpired to cause the breakup. I suggested this process to make you realize that you were actually both at fault, and it will take both of you to rebuild the relationship. Obviously, your previous relationship was beyond repair, and that is why you probably made it this far in this book. If you're considering starting with a fresh new face, then you need to prepare for it as follows: You must put aside all of your thoughts about women. Remember when I said that all women are not the same? Well, that still stands. Additionally, all women are not the cause of your past mistakes in your previous relationships. All negative attitudes must stay in the past, but keep what happened in your archives for reference just in case any of those signs show up in your new relationship. Don't pass on ill feelings that belong in the past. Get over it! You are starting out fresh, and it's possible that you have a good woman now, so don't ruin it.

Tips for a Successful New Relationship:

Don't misjudge — If you see something that you don't understand in your newfound friend, don't misjudge her actions or her moves. Always ask about it in a polite, respectful manner, and she just may tell you. You will feel like a heel if you see something about her, and you begin to have rude thoughts about her, only to find out it really wasn't what you thought in the first place. It also could be possible that you're not a good judge of character, so practice being nonjudgmental with her and ask when in doubt. If you can't ask her innocent questions, then you just may have the wrong friend.

Don't be quick to accuse — Don't be so quick to accuse your newfound friend about things you don't understand. I know I said in the earlier chapters not to be so trusting, but please have the common sense not to accuse her if you don't have solid proof.

Don't lie or engage in deceit — In your previous relationship, you told some lies and you probably deceived her. Do not bring that to the new friend in your life. You're starting out fresh, and if you have to lie and engage in deceit, then you don't have the right friend to start out with. You don't have to lie to keep her out of you private life. All you have to do is to say, "I don't want to rehash old wounds. I have to move on with my life. Maybe someday I'll tell you, but for now, that subject is closed." Now, if she keeps on pushing on the subject of your ex-relationship, then that is a strong sign that you should watch out, and your new friend will not last long with you. Her insistence that you talk about something sensitive you don't want to talk about is a strong sign that she is selfish, and that she isn't considering your need not to discuss it. Watch it!

Here are some thoughts and attitudes to keep in mind about yourself:

Don't be fickle — You are a grownup, and you should act like a man. It is important that you show this to a good and decent woman so that she can feel she can trust you. Even if you are having a hard time making up your mind, that is okay as long as you finally do make a decision. Deciding what you want and then changing your mind and deciding that you don't want it any more could be a strong sign that you don't know what you truly want out of life—or from a woman. If a woman finds this out about you, she will leave and you will have lost your chances. A good woman wants stability from a man, and to know that she doesn't have to babysit him. Nine times out of ten, her kids are grown, and she is looking for a good companion. She no longer wants to put up with child-like behavior. The only thing that I am telling you is, be sure and confident of your moves. If you are not, that's okay as long as you are analyzing the right way to accomplish your actions.

Don't engage in ungentlemanly behavior — Don't be the type of man who doesn't know how to be a gentleman. It is true that some men are extremely lazy in showing women that they are the right man for them. Don't let the female open her own door. When in a restaurant, don't order first and make her order afterwards. If your food comes first, wait for her food to come before you start eating. If you have to burp, then do so quietly then excuse yourself. You'd better not pass gas! Excuse yourself from the table and go into the restroom. When getting ready to leave, get up from the table and make sure you are there on her side to help her with her coat. If you're going for a walk, make sure you walk on the curbside, nearest to the traffic. These are good examples that you can follow every time you go out together. Practice these actions until they become your everyday routine. I have told you previously that, if you have a gentlemanly character, then you should embrace it. A real woman wants and needs a good gentleman to give her respect and acknowledge her dignity. Also a gentleman will not only open the doors for her, but also will give her attention when she ask for his attention. A gentleman will make sure she has everything that she wants before he goes out with the fellas. He may call her sometimes to see if she needs anything before he goes home for the evening. I think you get what I'm trying to tell you. These actions are the good characteristics of a gentleman.

Recognize domestic violence — Do you remember what I said in Chapter 3 about domestic violence? Now is the time to recognize the signs. All this time I have given you the signs of a dysfunctional person, and you should know if you display dysfunctional tendencies yourself. I also said that, if you are dysfunctional, then domestic violence is possible. You can downplay the situation all you want, but one thing is for sure domestic violence is domestic violence. Being quick tempered, cussing all the time, being ready to argue at all times, disagreeing and being ready to defend your beliefs—all of these are strong signs of being dysfunctional. Whether you see the signs in yourself or in your new friend, the signs are strong and undeniably dangerous. Sever the acquaintance immediately! If you carry this gene in you, then you're not ready for any relationship and you don't deserve a good decent woman.

Don't engage in masking — This is where you become an actor. You try to hide all of your flaws, and you try to hide your lifestyle as well. Sometimes a guy gives his friend's phone number to a woman and tries to start a relationship from there on. Sometimes a guy never wants the female to see where he lives. Okay, that might work during weeks one through three, but you don't try to hide things you don't want her to see unless your motives are sinister in the first place. If they are, then you've got no business with this book, and you need to give it to a real man, seriously. Note: If you use the information in this book for ulterior motives, then I pray the females who are real women see your game and stop you in your tracks.

Thoughts and Attitudes to Keep in Mind About You and Your New Friend

Make doable plans— I strongly advise you to take your date to a real sit-down restaurant. If this is a dinner date, then make sure you plan something that she will like as much as you do. Don't be selfish. Remember, you want to make a good impression, so plan the right evening. Leave your bad habits at home and bring your amazing skills and respectful actions with you. If you make the plans, then you pay. If she makes the plans, then she should pay. Don't let a female tell you how to spend your money. Now, if she says she is paying, then that's okay, but you could be a gentleman and offer to pay. You're just being nice, that's all. Whatever you do, don't spend a lot of money. Remember, she is only a friend, and she doesn't hold the honorable title of "girlfriend" or "wife." Even then, watch how much money you spend. Remember what I said about being materialistic? It can destroy a relationship—especially a new one.

See how she acts— Now keep in mind that you are still in the beginning stages of the dating period. What I am about to say should still be done during weeks one through three. Take notice if she always has excuses about why she can't do something. You need to also take notice if she is complicated or high maintenance. If she is one of these characters, then you are seriously in trouble. You're not going to be able to keep up with her, you're not going to be able to lead a normal life with her, and you're going to work hard only to feed her flighty needs. You certainly don't need that type of responsibility. Not only that, she may ask for money because she doesn't want to spend her own. As I said before, you have yet to make a formal commitment with her.

Keep your eyes open to see if she is a positive person. If she is a positive person, then that is a good thing for you. Now, please don't get me wrong—a person can be too positive, and that can be a problem as well. Let me explain what I mean. All this time I have been saying that it is good to have a positive person, but if the person is too positive, he or she can drive you nuts. A person who is too positive doesn't look at the negative side of a situation at all. She has what you might guess—strong tunnel vision. Here's an example: Let's take a look at a female who is making plans for her wedding day. Her name is Rayna. Rayna is planning an outdoor wedding. She is what one would call a positive person, but she has a flaw, and that is she is *too* positive. She has finished with her wedding plans, and made the payments on time; however, she didn't make alternate plans in case it rains on her wedding day. So her friends and family ask, "What if it rains?" Rayna just smiles and says, "It won't rain. It's my wedding day!" So the day before the wedding is hectic, and Rayna's mother asks her, "What will we do if it rains? Shouldn't we make plans to have it inside too? It isn't too late." Rayna states that it's not going to rain. Looking at the sky, she sees no clouds anywhere. "The weatherman says there is a sixty percent chance of rain for tomorrow," Rayna's mother explains. Rayna doesn't change her mind. Well, it's the day of the wedding, and the sky is beautiful. The wedding is set for noon. As everything is being prepared for the outside wedding, the clouds start rolling in. At 10:30 in the morning, sprinkles arrive. Rayna's mother runs to her daughter to say it's sprinkling. "No worries," says the bride. "It's going to stop." At noon, no one is outside; everything is ruined by the rain, and Rayna is upstairs crying her eyes out.

I gave you this example because similar situations really do happen. Being overly positive can makes a person engage in stupid behavior. These people can make your life unbearable.

If she has children, make sure she isn't trying to make you support them — Believe it or not, there are females who will play the game of trying to get a man with a good job to help them financially with the kids. Don't get caught up in something you may have trouble getting out of. Don't be relaxed, and don't be naïve. It may take longer than three weeks to see where she's coming from.

Make sure she isn't always trying to spend your money — You will want to watch out for this also. You need to analyze these characteristics for more than three weeks (if you stay with her that long). Some females are quick to spend your money, and some actually use common sense. Just watch out for those gold diggers. Remember, a woman's anatomy isn't everything.

Avoid unnecessary babies — If you're having sex, then use protection no matter what she says. Do not trust her when she says she's taking protection. Many females lie, and then the next thing you know she is pregnant. Your life has been changed forever, all because you didn't play it smart. You may get some females who say they can't tolerate condoms. If that is the case, then they have no business having sex. Just play it smart and don't make any unnecessary babies.

Are you checking your character? (Things to fix within yourself)

While you are exploring your relationship with your newfound friend, are you checking your own character? Now I know that you may not be doing that, but you really should be checking how you treat a woman. Here is a list you can use to check your behavior. If you find anything that needs to be fixed, just take the time and fix it. The answers to these questions will help you identify potential problems that could arise in your new relationship.

- Are you a difficult man to be with?
- Are you a promoter of domestic violence?
- Are you a dysfunctional person?

- Do you always put your parents first before any relationship you're in?
- Are you a bullheaded person who goes against doing the right things in life?
- Are you always at your ex-partner's beckon and call?
- Are you henpecked?
- Do you have playmates you can't do without?
- Are you friends with destructive females?

These questions reflect situations that can continue to ruin your life as well as your new friend's life. You need to get rid of any negative influences before they become permanent in your life. Now the one point I want to explain is the one about your parents: "Do you always put your parents first before any relationship you're in?" In some cases, a man's parents don't want him to have anyone in his life because they feel that the woman that he is fond of is taking him away from them. So, to please them, he takes care of his parent's needs at all times. A man who has a relationship like that with his parents will never have a personal relationship with a woman. I must also say that there may not be a woman out here who would stand for that.

Chapter 16

The Assessment
(Weeks Four through Eight)

Have you made a decision about your new friend? I have prepared a special checklist for your convenience that you can use to assist you in analyzing your friend. A word of advice—do not overlook anything that you see in your friend that isn't sitting with you well. If there is an issue that is disturbing you, then you need to consider it seriously. Before you begin to analyze your friend's character, you need to get a sheet of paper and set up two columns. Label the first column "I can live with this" and label the second column "I can't live with this." Record your *answers* to the questions under these headings. This method is important; it can prevent you from making a mistake in accepting something you can't live with. Let the checklist guide you in the right direction. It's good also to ask your own questions; they may be even more helpful in making a decision. Just let the questions I have supplied serve as guidelines as your analysis. Here are my questions:

- Is she a decent woman?
- Is she a decent woman with a complicated life?
- Is she a decent woman who has to be shown what a real relationship is?
- Is this woman worth your time?
- Is sex complicating my decision?
- Is your new friend a decent woman who always wants her way?
- How many times has she called you?
- How many times have you called her?

- Do either of you drink alcohol? If you do, do you remain respectful to each other?
- Are you going to proceed with her? If you are, do you think you are both ready to take the relationship to the next level?

Note: Do not let tunnel vision cause you to make the wrong decision. Be honest about your true feelings, and just take it slow if she is worth it.

Chapter 17

Proceeding to the Next Level

If you both decide to make a go of it, then you need to agree at the same time to move forward. This is no time for mixed signals, which means that both of you have to be on the same page. Remember to keep games out of the equation and make sure she understands where you are coming from. You must speak to her, and you both must come to a positive agreement about the next level you are about to enter together. It's important both of you to avoid involving games, ex-partners, ex-playmates, family members, friends and strangers. If you are going to make this work, then you both must have the major ingredients for a good solid base: respect, understanding, communication, compromising and love.

Because it is still early in the relationship, you will always have to pay attention to emotions. Tempers can flare, but it will be the responsibility of both of you to keep it in check. I want to remind you of something I said in the earlier chapters, and that is, just because you know how to please a woman, that doesn't mean you know how to please *all* women. Please remember that all women are not the same, so don't walk into this next level thinking you know this female. Find out what she likes, and then proceed to obtain it. (But make sure she isn't expecting it.)

Teach her how you want to be treated and respected. The only way she is going to learn how you want to be treated is for you to tell her. Then, after you tell her, show her during the following weeks. Now, keep in mind that she will, hopefully, do the same to you. She should be telling you how she wants to be treated and respected as well. If she doesn't, then she is beginning to play games. You have to train each other until each understands the other's expectations. So the main question is, how will either of you know what the other expects if it isn't explained? I truly believe this makes a lot of sense, and I hope you totally agree.

Domestic violence is one of the most dangerous situations to be in. I have talked about this in earlier chapters, and I told you how to recognize the potential for domestic violence in her as well as in yourself. Now is the time to sever the relationship if you see even the smallest signs of it in her. One thing I need to stress to you is that you must have the type of mate or friend who will bring out the best in you. You've already had a mate who brought out the worst in you, so don't let it happen again. A dysfunctional person will bring out the worst in you, and you will live in domestic violence for the length of the relationship. So my final advice is to keep domestic violence out of your relationship and out of your life.

Chapter 18

What a decent woman wants in a man.

Treatment is Everything

A good, decent woman wants to be noticed by her man. She wants him to notice the things that she does that are positive. She wants him to show her love and admiration. A decent woman wants security and stability from her man. She wants to find other reasons to fall deeper in love with him as she hopes that he doesn't destroy her heart. A good woman wants her man to show appreciation that she is in his life. She is happy when her man respects her, and she will respect him as well. She wants to be able to come to him and have a good conversation with him. She wants to have the courage to love him without the drama some relationships have. A good woman wants to have strong confidence in her man without being deceived by him. A good, decent woman wants her man to be able to take care of problems in a positive way. She doesn't want false hopes from him, and she wants him to be able to lead the relationship in a positive manner. She wants both of you to work as a positive team. Most of all, she wants her mate to protect her in life unconditionally.

Don't Keep Up Appearances

One way to lose your new friend is to be something you're not. The best way for you to be is to be yourself. Let her fall for the real you. Don't do things you don't normally do. Impress her by doing the things that she wants, and make sure it is something that you do all the time. Also, don't act in ways you don't normally act. A woman hates it when a man is fake, and that is another good way to lose her as well. If you act normally in the beginning, you don't have to keep up fake appearances. A woman who is good and true will give you all the love she can give. She will be there for you at all times. A woman's love can be unconditional, and I advise you strongly not to deceive her in any way. I have told many men that, if they want a good woman, they need to learn how to treat her. If you become friends with a decent woman, don't act like you don't know how to treat her. You will certainly lose her forever.

Chapter 19

Female Predators
(They Are Real and Active)

A female predator will act like the prefect woman for you. She will do the things that you feel a woman should do. These females will play the role of the perfect female until they have no more use for you. They can have more than one victim at a time and make you think you're the only one. One of the main reasons a predator will come to you is to see if you have any money, property, and a good job. Her goal is to live the high life and have you take care of her. Period. She will be fake in everything she does; her love for you will even be fake. Only you will be able to tell if she is a fake or not. You will know by keeping your guard up as I have told you to do. This female predatory will give you fake stability, and most of all, everything this female does will be a lie. She will make you think you are the only one and you're not. She will make your whole relationship a lie. This female predator will give you false hopes, and you won't be able to see it until it's too late and the damage is done. She will stay with you as long as it takes to rip you off, and please know the more you have the more she will be after.

If you use an online dating site, you are taking a big gamble, as those sites are loaded with female predators. You will not be able to tell by their photos and profiles if they are lying or not. If you are lonely, you will be more of a victim. They can post pictures of other women instead of themselves, or they can post pictures taken when they were younger. Please don't be foolish like the men who have fallen for these females. If you are gullible, then you can fall for them as well. No matter what type of game you think you can play, they will be better at it than you are. So my advice to you is to stay out of those dating sites unless you really know what you are doing, and you know how to take precaution.

Chapter 20

Are You Really Ready for Marriage?

If you are thinking about marrying that special female who has gone with you through that special journey, then you need to get ready for that as well. Marriage is a big step for any man to take. You should go through with it only if you feel you're ready. You must also make sure your partner is ready. If she isn't ready and you are, a complicated situation could develop. Marriage is a big step and shouldn't be taken lightly. If you both live by yourselves, living together will be a big adjustment. To live with someone 24/7, 365 days a year can be a bit much. Living with each other's faults can cause ill feelings between the both of you. Love isn't going to be enough. Just because you love someone, that doesn't mean you can live with her. Not only that, remembering to report your comings and goings be difficult at first. Then there are questions about how each of you will help around the house. I can go on and on, but I think you get the picture.

If you've thought about these situations and you think you are ready to deal with them, then you need to start thinking about who are you marrying—her or her family? Who is going to be in control of your marriage—you as a couple, or your families? Did you set the rules for having children? Are the both of you willing to compromise? What will be your time limits? Do you know that you both still have to work to maintain the relationship? Last but not least, can each of you live with the other's faults? These questions are serious; the answers can make or break a marriage. All these questions and more need to be explored before you walk down that aisle together.

If you have made the decision to be married, then congratulations on your decision! I wish the best for both of you.

Please remember that you must act as team together, and you should keep other people out of your relationship. When I say others, I mean your friends and family members. Don't give your friends and family members reports on how things are going. I highly recommend that you both keep your mouths closed. What happens between you and your wife stays between you and your wife (unless domestic violence is involved). It is in your best interest to be careful whom you take advice from. Just remember what I disclosed to you in the earlier chapters about talking to your friends and family members. If you have forgotten, then please go back and read the chapters again. Please use common sense. If you are married, then you can't do the same things single men do. You have started a new lifestyle, and you have to grow up and be a real married man. Let me advise you that, if you go to a gentleman's club, that says a lot to a wife or girlfriend, so watch what you do.

Now, if you have had other women in your life, then you need to lose them quickly. If you can't do without them, then you have no business being married. I'm talking about the women who are your friends, especially those who come with benefits (you know what I mean). Stop all of your flirting with your previous female companions. Change your phone number, and don't let any of those females near your new life. Now, if by some chance you see something in your wife's life like another man, ask her about him with caution. Keep in mind that what I'm talking about should have been discussed before the marriage.

As usual, always keep your eyes and ears open to what is going on in your relationship. I have given you knowledge and ideas about what could happen, and I have taught you what to do and what not to do. Of course there is a lot more to what I'm saying about good, decent women. Women aren't so hard to understand. Just tell them what you expect, and don't let any woman run over you. Be a man, and tell her that, if she is upset, then she must talk about what is bothering her. She should never expect you to have to figure out why she is upset. You have the power to make her stop. If she carries the anger for more than a day, then you have an issue on your hands. Train her to stop that nonsense and talk to you. If she keeps doing it, then she needs to move on. But if she really loves you, then she will comply. And you should follow the same rules for yourself. Good luck in your knowledge of *Want a Real Woman Wants, What a Real Woman Needs.*

Food For Thought

Now, I trust that you gentleman have read this book from front to back. I wanted to save this part for last because I know how some men are. I have encountered some men who do not like to read certain books, and in their opinion, they feel it takes too long to get to the point. Well, for the men who feel this way, I have this to tell you: If you had the knowledge in the first place on how to treat a woman, then there wouldn't be a problem. To defend yourselves with regard to your actions, the first thing you usually say is that women are hard to get along with, or women always play games, or there is no getting along with women. I have heard men talking badly about women. Now, let me say something to the ones who are complaining about women: Men have a bad habit of doing something wrong, then not owning up to what they have done. Please understand that not all men do this, but there are a lot who do. Now, I am not talking about women, and if you want to know what I have said about women, then you need to purchase my book, *A New Beginning: A Woman's Guide to Self-Respect in Order to Make a Stand.*

If you are one of the men who understand what I have told them in this publication, then you may know what I'm about to say in this section. One thing for sure is that men have always picked the wrong women for themselves, and they go through hell trying to get out of these relationships. Men do some of the craziest things in order to get out of any bad situation. Yes, there are some men who are victims of domestic violence—the female is the culprit. You don't hear that much about it because society would laugh at the situation. The first thing some people might say, "You let that woman beat you up, and you're a man?" Then here comes the laughter as these men are ridiculed. The truth is, there is nothing funny about it. Men go through depression, property destruction, and other aspects of domestic violence. The men who go through these problems are the ones who picked the wrong females. In this book, I have shown you the right way to pick a woman. It isn't easy, and that is why it is important to take your time in choosing the right female.

Those men who do wrong things and don't want the females to say anything about it must stop now. Remember what I have said in the earlier chapters? A mistake is an action in which you didn't know what you were doing. If you do something intentionally, and you know the outcome, then the action is *not* a mistake. Stop playing games and grow up! If you want a good and decent woman, then you need to get with the program and show her that you deserve her presents. Don't align yourself with a woman so you can take advantage of her. Women these days do not tolerate the games men play.

If you feel that there is too much to do to find the right woman, then you really don't need this book, and you need to pass it to a man who is willing to make his life better. As always, nothing is guaranteed in life, but you can take steps to make sure your life is more positive. I want you to think of searching for the right woman the way you think of searching for your favorite car to buy, or working on your favorite hobbies. You put a great deal of time and effort into purchasing a good car as well as enjoying your hobbies—you just won't settle for something mediocre. Well, you should apply those same feelings to your search for a good mate, and remember that it won't happen unless you try. I wish you the best in your search for a good mate. Remember to be careful, be safe, and be blessed.

About the Author

Madena Williams started her writing career in junior high school. Using her life's experience in her publications, she has managed to teach others how to cope, survive, and triumph over everyday problems in relationships. Seeing her ability, both men and women seek her advice on overcoming domestic violence. Madena Williams is currently a domestic violence survivor of thirty-five years and counting. Residing in Michigan with her family, she is a motivational and inspirational teacher of everyday life.